The Little Book of Prosperity

Prosperity is *Simply a Choice*

Praise for the *Little Book of Prosperity*

"The truth is always simpler than theory, and a little book may contain more truth than several big ones. Keep this one near you — it will help bring you back to insight and balance each time you open it."

—Fredric Lehrman, Director of Nomad University, creator of *"Prosperity Consciousness"* audio series

"If you're ready for prosperity, or more prosperity, read this little book now."

—Mark Victor Hansen, co-creator of *Chicken Soup for the Soul*

"The surprisingly simple and yet highly effective concepts, tools, and strategies that you will discover in this book have the power to transform your financial life forever. This is the kind of book you'll want to read over and over, and give copies to your family and friends."

—Raymond Aaron, *NY Times* bestselling author of *Double Your Income Doing What You Love*

The Little Book of Prosperity

Prosperity is *Simply a Choice*

PJ Van Hulle

OUR little BOOKS

ISBN 978-1-935157-12-0

The publication is designed to provide accurate and authoritative information in regard to the subject matter covered. It is sold with the understanding that the Publisher is not engaged in rendering legal, medical, accounting or other professional services. If legal or medical advice or other expert assistance is required, the services of a competent professional person should be sought. This book is not intended to treat or diagnose any medical condition and does not substitute for medical treatment. For any health difficulties and for on-going care, please see your physician, psychotherapist or other licensed medical professional.

Illustration by Bryan Fitzgerald
www.ourlittlebooks.com
E-mail: sales@ourlittlebooks.com
Printed in Canada.

Contents

Prosperity is Simply a Choice

"Abundance is not something we acquire.
It is something we tune into."
—Wayne Dyer

Welcome to the *Little Book of Prosperity*. The purpose of this book is to support you in tapping into the prosperity and abundance you desire. Every time you read this book, you will gain new insights, awareness, and inspiration.

This book is not a story with a beginning, middle and end. It's a collection of tools, ideas, and strategies for creating wealth and happiness in your life. You can open it to any chapter at random and receive the benefit.

Have you ever noticed that prosperity and wealth seem to come easily to some people, while others continue to struggle, no matter how smart they are or how hard they work? You are about to discover powerful concepts, tools and strategies for naturally attracting more prosperity and wealth into your life.

Most people don't use the word "prosperity" in conversation. You probably hear people talking about wanting to make more money or wanting to be rich. However, when people think they want more money, what they actually want is the experience that they think more money will give them, whether that's happiness, peace of mind, or freedom. That experience is the experience of prosperity.

The first step in choosing prosperity is to realize that if you are reading this book, you are already wealthier than 95 percent of the world's population.

Think about it. Would you trade financial lives with someone else on the planet who was chosen at random? If you're lucky, you could end up with an extremely wealthy person, a Bill Gates or a Richard Branson. However, the odds are that you would end up with a far lower standard of living than what you have now.

Factor time into the equation. Would you trade places with a king or a queen who lived 300 years ago? To "live like a king" sounds great, since that was then the most lavish lifestyle possible. You would enjoy feasts and be waited on by servants; however, you would not have running water, electricity, phones, antibiotics, the Internet, airplanes, or any of the other modern conveniences that we take for granted.

You're already beginning to feel more wealthy and prosperous, aren't you?

Why Most People Don't Get What They Want (And How You Can)

> *"The first step to getting the things you want out of life is this: Decide what you want."*
>
> —Ben Stein

The Number One reason that most people don't get what they want is, they don't ***know*** what they want.

You obviously like the idea of prosperity or you wouldn't be reading this book, right? But what does prosperity mean to you specifically? And how will you know when you have it?

It's so important to define what prosperity means *to you* so that you know what you're going for and will know when you have achieved it. Otherwise, it's like playing a game with no rules. How will you know when you're winning?

According to popular minister and author Eric Butterworth:

"Prosperity is a way of living and thinking, and not just money or things. Poverty is a way of living and thinking, and not just a lack of money or things."

The dictionary definition of prosperity is: the state of flourishing, thriving, success, or good fortune. Prosperity often encompasses wealth, but also includes other factors, such as happiness and health.

Fredric Lehrman, creator of the Prosperity Consciousness course offered by Nightingale-Conant defines prosperity as, "The experience of functioning effortlessly and conveniently in the physical universe, whether you have money or not."

It's also important to ask yourself: Do you <u>really</u> want to be wealthy?

If so, how do you define wealth?

How much money would you need to have to consider yourself wealthy? An annual income of $100,000 per year? A net worth of $5,000,000? The definition of wealth is completely subjective, different for each individual, and probably changes for you over time.

The word "wealth" comes from the Old English word "weal," which means "well-being."

When you say you want to be wealthy, what you are really saying is that you want to experience well-being. You don't want the actual dollars; you want the experience that you believe those dollars will bring you.

To me, prosperity is the experience of feeling grateful for the abundance that's in your life right now AND looking forward to even more abundance.

When you cultivate that way of thinking and living, isn't it easier to attract more wealth than when you're living in scarcity and fear?

Wealth Secrets of Cherry Blossoms

"Live every day as if it were your last and then some day you'll be right."
—H.H. "Breaker" Morant

It's not an accident that cherry blossoms are on the cover of this book. They serve as a visual reminder to readers to appreciate how precious life is and to choose prosperity in *all* aspects of life.

Since medieval times, cherry blossoms have been an important symbol in the warrior code and in Buddhism because they're so delicate, beautiful and short-lived.

Cherry blossoms are a powerful metaphor for life. Sometime between late March and early April, the blossoms open all at once; their petals fall in seven-to-ten days.

I enjoyed two magnificent cherry blossom seasons when I lived and taught in Japan. One winter morning in Japan, as I was preparing to teach a class, my mom called.

"Your grandpa isn't doing well. We think he's going to die. Come home now."

I had tickets to go home for Christmas in two weeks. So I called my grandma, who said, "Everything is fine. You don't have to come now."

At that point, I was really confused. Do I go? Do I wait? What's really going on? I decided to go, as I was very close to my grandpa.

I was able to get on a plane that day.

When I arrived at my grandparents' house, Gramps was sitting alone in the living room. He hugged me and said, "Oh, Dolly, thank God you're here!"

He died twelve hours later.

Flying home early was one of the best decisions I've ever made. I was able to be with my grandpa and say goodbye while he was still alive.

How often we get caught up in day-to-day routines, irritations, and to-do lists and miss potentially life-changing moments!

Life is beautiful, precious, and too short to waste in scrambling paycheck to paycheck. When it comes right down to it, what really matters to you?

This book is about creating the life you CHOOSE to live, creating prosperity in all aspects of your life.

Just as cherry blossoms have five petals, there are five main aspects of leading a prosperous life:

Emotional
Physical
Mental
Spiritual
Financial

Each "petal" affects the others. For example, some people focus only on making money and allow their health and relationships to suffer. Many couples end up fighting about money. By using this holistic approach to finances, you can have a rich and fulfilling life, not just a lot of money (although it's perfectly acceptable to ALSO have a lot of money). In the upcoming chapters, you will also discover more information about each of these tips.

Emotional Prosperity

Emotional prosperity means enjoying fulfilling relationships with others and with yourself. Here are some ideas for increasing your emotional prosperity:

1. Schedule "You Time"
2. Schedule "Date Night" with Your Partner, Family or Friends
3. Take a Vacation

Write down your thoughts on how to increase your Emotional Prosperity.

Physical Prosperity

Physical prosperity means taking care of your body and experiencing vibrant health and vitality. Here are some ideas for increasing your physical prosperity:

1. Work Out (Find Something You Really Enjoy)
2. Eat Healthy, Nutritious Foods
3. Get Enough Sleep

Write down your thoughts on how to increase your Physical Prosperity.

Mental Prosperity

Mental prosperity means being a life-long learner and staying mentally sharp. Here are some ideas for increasing your mental prosperity:

1. Read for 15 Minutes a Day
2. Do Puzzles like Sudoku
3. Take Classes and Attend Seminars

Write down your thoughts on how to increase your Mental Prosperity.

Spiritual Prosperity

Spiritual prosperity means feeling connected to your unique personal experience of spirit, whatever that looks like for you and whatever you call it. Here are some ideas for increasing your spiritual prosperity:

1. Invest 15 Minutes a Day in Prayer or Meditation
2. Write in a Journal
3. Attend a Spiritual Gathering

Write down your thoughts on how to increase your Spiritual Prosperity.

Financial Prosperity

Financial prosperity means not having to depend on a job, a spouse, the government, or anyone else for money. Here are some ideas for increasing your financial prosperity.

1. Have a Regular "Money Date"
2. Open and Maintain Your Permanent Wealth Account
3. Increase Your Financial Education

Write down your thoughts on how to increase your Financial Prosperity.

Your Relationship with Money

> *"Let's set the record straight. Money is important! To say that it's not as important as any other things in life is ludicrous. What's more important, your arm or your leg? Could it be that both are important?"*
>
> —T. Harv Eker

Just like you have relationships with other people, you have a relationship with money. First, decide that your money is important to you and worth spending time with. If you're in a relationship with someone and you tell them "you're just not that important to me," how long do you think they're going to stick around?

Do you keep your cash organized in your wallet, or crumpled up in wads around the house with piles of loose change? I encourage you to treat your money with respect.

When money is important to you, you are willing to spend quality time with your money, just like with someone you're dating. Schedule a regular time to give your money your full attention.

During your "Money Date," you can find out how your money is doing by reviewing your financial statements, balancing your checkbook, or reconciling your accounts.

In the past, when I didn't have a regular "Money Date," I handled my finances randomly. I would balance my checkbook and pay bills when I got around to it, which meant that sometimes I was organized and sometimes my finances were in total chaos. I wasted hundreds of dollars in fees that could have been avoided if I was monitoring my finances more closely.

Now that I have regular and consistent "Money Dates," I have clarity around my finances, and I make better decisions. I love that, and I believe you will, too.

What They Didn't Teach You about Money in School

> *"Academic qualifications are important and so is financial education. They're both important, and schools are forgetting one of them."*
>
> —Robert Kiyosaki

If you're reading this book, you've probably had some form of formal education, whether it was high school, college, or even just grade school. What did they teach you about money in school? If you're like the thousands of other people I've worked with, the answer is "not much."

If you're not going to learn about money in school, how do you get a FINANCIAL EDUCATION?

By “financial education,” I’m talking specifically about how to make, save, manage, invest, and protect your money.

Make
Save
Manage
Invest
Protect

Pretend that your part-time job is managing your money and watching your wealth grow. (Some fantastic resources for increasing your financial education are listed in the “PJ Recommends” section at the back of this book.)

Your Permanent Wealth Account

"I found the road to wealth when I decided that a part of all I earned was mine to keep."
—George S. Clason,
The Richest Man in Babylon

How much money has flowed through your life? How much have you kept? If you haven't kept very much money, that's because you didn't have a structure — until now.

In his Prosperity Consciousness course, Fredric Lehrman invites you to imagine living in a time before bank accounts, checkbooks, and even printed currency. See yourself carrying around a leather pouch and receiving your income in the form of ten gold coins.

You buy shoes. You eat. Eventually your pouch is empty and you work in order to get ten more gold coins. Your pouch fills and empties and fills and empties — a natural ebb and flow. Most people spend as much as they make; so when their income goes up, so do their expenses.

Now imagine that you have a SECOND POUCH. And every time you put ten gold coins in the first pouch, you immediately take one coin and move it to the second pouch. You continue to add and subtract from the first pouch, but you NEVER spend the coins in the second pouch. Eventually the second pouch would become too heavy to carry around.

This is the idea of the permanent wealth account.

Open a bank account that is completely separate from all your other accounts with the sole intention of putting money in there and never ever touching the principal.

Remember the story of the goose that laid the golden eggs? You would never kill that goose, would you? You'd want to live off the golden eggs. Well, the permanent wealth account is your Golden Goose.

Having a permanent wealth account is like having your own Golden Goose.

Having this account reinforces two very important beliefs.

Belief #1 — "I have money."

What you focus on expands. If you're always complaining about how you're broke and have no money, it's hard to attract money to you.

On the other hand, it's easy to receive more of what you already have. So if you already have money, it's easy to attract more.

Belief #2 — "I have more money than I'll ever need."

What an abundant belief! You'll never touch the principal, which means that you do have more money than you'll ever need.

In my experience, the amount of money in my permanent wealth account moves easily in my life. It's like a magnet for more money. When I got to $10,000, I found it easier to attract another $10,000.

It's easy to calculate 10 percent of your income. And it's easy to live off 90 percent of your income. You won't even notice the 10 percent is gone, as long as you pay yourself first.

You MUST **pay yourself first**!!! Otherwise, that 10 percent will get spent. Every time you receive a check, automatically transfer 10 percent into your permanent wealth account. Do this until it becomes an automatic habit for you.

If you don't have any income, start by contributing whatever you can. The practice of managing your money is more important than the amount.

You'll have so much fun with this account that you'll want to contribute even more money. Having fun is important! Start by putting aside 10 percent of your income, and soon you'll contribute even more.

How to Stop Worrying about Money

> *"If you can't sleep, then get up and do something instead of lying there worrying. It's the worry that gets you, not the lack of sleep."*
>
> —Dale Carnegie

When you are feeling worried and stressed, you are not having the experience of living in prosperity. Some harmful effects of stress are anxiety, depression, heart disease, sleep problems, and weight gain. Please don't waste your energy stressing about money.

Here is a simple three-step process for HOW to turn stress into creativity and prosperity.

First of all, in order for this to work, you need to be aware that you're feeling stressed. Awareness is the first step in change.

Next, realize that every thought has a psychosomatic response in the body. What this means is that when you think something, it affects your body and feelings. Imagine taking a big sip of pure lemon juice. Don't you feel your jaw tighten?

If you're feeling stress in your body, your thinking is causing you to feel stressed. Therefore, the first step in eliminating stress is to identify that thought.

Next, you can consciously switch to a thought that feels better and programs you to make more money and be more creative.

The process is:

1. Awareness
2. Identify the Thought
3. Switch the Thought

For example, one stressful thought may be:

"I Can't Afford It."

When you say "I can't afford it," your mind shuts down. Henry Ford said, "Whether you think you can or whether you think you can't, you're right."

What if you switched that thought to:

"How Can I Afford It?"

When you ask "How can I?" your mind automatically goes searching for answers to that question. You've successfully changed your stress into creativity.

The Fastest and Easiest Path to Prosperity

"Gratitude is riches. Complaint is poverty."
—Doris Day

The fastest and easiest way to tune into prosperity is to get into an emotional state of gratitude.

Gratitude is an extremely powerful emotion. Robert A. Emmons from the University of California-Davis and Michael E. McCullough from the University of Miami conducted a long-term research project designed to study the effects of gratitude. Here are some of their findings:

- In an experimental comparison, those who kept gratitude journals on a weekly basis exercised more regularly, reported fewer physical symptoms, felt better about their lives as a whole, and were more optimistic about the upcoming week compared to those who recorded hassles or neutral life events.

- Participants who kept gratitude lists were more likely to have made progress toward important personal goals over a two-month period compared to subjects in the other experimental conditions.

- In a sample of adults with neuromuscular disease, a 21-day gratitude intervention resulted in greater amounts of high-energy positive moods, a greater sense of feeling connected to others, more optimistic ratings of one's life, and better sleep duration and sleep quality, relative to a control group.

- Grateful people report higher levels of positive emotions, life satisfaction, vitality and optimism and lower levels of depression and stress. The disposition toward gratitude appears to enhance pleasant-feeling states more than it diminishes unpleasant emotions. Grateful people do not deny or ignore the negative aspects of life.

- People with a strong disposition toward gratitude have the capacity to be empathic and to take the perspective of others. They are rated as more generous and more helpful by people in their social networks.

The simplest and fastest way to tap into your feelings of gratitude is a process to make a list of people, pets, places, things, and experiences that you are grateful for. You can do this mentally or out loud. I've found that it's most effective for me when I write it down.

A highly beneficial practice is to keep a gratitude journal. Every night before you go to bed, write down five things that you're grateful for.

Use this space to write down what you are grateful for:

How to Turn Irritation into Gratitude

"When you focus on the goodness in your life, you create more of it. Opportunities, relationships, even money flowed my way when I learned to be grateful no matter what happened in my life."

—Oprah Winfrey

If you're reading this book, you are already a relatively positive thinker. Otherwise, you wouldn't have attracted this information. You already ARE grateful for your life.

It's not the big things that knock you off-course. It's the little day-to-day stresses and irritations that trip you up and disconnect you from your natural state of prosperity. You're totally enlightened until someone cuts you off in traffic.

Here's how to turn that feeling of irritation or frustration into gratitude and thereby attract more prosperity.

Ask yourself: "Who would be grateful to have this problem?"

If you're irritated about being stuck in traffic, think of people who don't own cars or who can't drive or who have such boring lives that they have no place to go.

If you're annoyed by your glasses or contact lenses, think of someone who is blind.

If your spouse is annoying you, think about someone who wanted to get married and never did, or someone whose spouse has died and is lonely, or someone who got divorced and regrets it.

Do this until the frustration subsides and you begin to feel grateful.

How to Get Rid of Stuck Energy

> *"Clutter is stuck energy. The word "clutter" derives from the Middle English word "clotter," which means to coagulate — and that's about as stuck as you can get."*
>
> —Karen Kingston,
> *Clear Your Clutter with Feng Shui*

You can instantly begin to feel more prosperous by clearing the clutter in your life. As you clear your clutter, you will begin to experience higher levels of energy, clarity and well-being. Remember that the word "wealth" gets its origins from the word for "well-being."

Clutter is a low, stagnant and chaotic energy that drains your energy. Feng Shui practitioners will tell you that clutter can also negatively influence or even block the flow of events in specific areas of your life.

You may have been procrastinating on cleaning your clutter because you think you don't have the time, but actually you know on an instinctive level that clearing clutter can be an emotional process, and if you just set a timer for 20 minutes and GET STARTED, you will begin making progress and feeling great about yourself right away.

Once you set your timer, you can focus on clearing one area at a time.

Here's a checklist to get you started:

____ Clear the clutter under the bed

____ Clean out the refrigerator

____ Clean out and organize a drawer

____ Clean out and organize another drawer

____ Find pens that no longer work and throw them away

____ Create a neat “inbox” for your incoming mail

____ Pick up any change you find around the house and put it into your permanent wealth account

____ De-hoard your closets. Let go of as many items as possible that no longer fit or you haven’t used in a long time.

Zapping Tolerations

"The sculptor produces the beautiful statue by chipping away such parts of the marble block as are not needed — it is a process of elimination."

—Elbert Hubbard

Tolerations are whatever you've been tolerating or procrastinating about that drains your energy — a messy desk, a task that has been on your "to-do" list for months, a friend who likes to complain a lot.

Tolerations can refer to annoying things, small inconveniences, your own behavior or the behavior of others. They deplete your energy, waste your time, and get in the way of you leading a prosperous and happy life.

Here are some ways you can zap tolerations:

- Cancel monthly bills for things you don't use
- Ask yourself what other expenses you can eliminate
- Clear clutter
- Have a conversation that you've been avoiding
- Fix that leaky faucet
- Work on changing your own habits
- Create a plan to pay off high-interest credit card debt

Make a list of all the tolerations that have been draining your energy and start "zapping" them by resolving them one by one. You don't have to eliminate all of them at once. You can enroll other people to help you tackle them, especially the larger projects, like cleaning out the garage. You will be amazed at how much more energetic, alive, and happy you feel as you zap more and more tolerations. If there are some that you simply have no idea how to zap, re-read the section on turning irritation into gratitude.

Imagine having a totally clean and organized home and office, satisfying relationships with family, co-workers and friends, and no debt. Don't you feel more prosperous already?

Use this space to list tolerations you are ready to zap:

Learning the Language of Prosperity

"'Careful with fire' is good advice, we know.
'Careful with words' is ten times doubly so."
—William Carleton

Just as you can learn Spanish or Japanese, there is a specific language of prosperity. Once you become fluent in that language, you will naturally attract more prosperity into your life.

The words you speak create your reality.

First of all, anytime you say "I am," you are programming yourself by giving your subconscious mind a command. When someone asks you, "How are you?" you have an opportunity to program yourself.

If you say "I'm OK" on a regular basis, you will have just an OK life. When you answer "I'm fantastic!" that is the beginning of having a fantastic life. Test this out. When you say "I'm fantastic," see if you immediately start to feel more fantastic and have more energy. If you feel fantastic and energized, it's so much easier to make money.

The language of prosperity is a language of power. There is no place for wimpy words like "if" or "try" or "but." Instead of "if," say "when." If I have the money, I'll take a vacation becomes "When I have the money, I'll take a vacation." And, as Yoda says in *Star Wars*, "Do or do not. There is no try." Say "I will," or, "My plan is to…" The word "but" negates what you said before, for example, if you tell someone, "I love you, but…" Replace "but" with "and."

If	→	When
Try	→	Will
But	→	And
Can't	→	How Can I?

Finally, eliminate "I can't" from your vocabulary. When you say "I can't," your mind immediately shuts down. "I can't" really only means one of two things… either "I don't want to" or "I don't know how." If you don't want to, just own that. If you don't know how, then the question becomes "How can I?"

Instead of saying "I can't reach my goal," ask yourself, "How can I reach my goal?"

Instead of saying "I can't afford it," ask yourself, "How can I afford it?"

How to Turn Failure into Success

> *"Success is going from failure to failure without losing enthusiasm."*
>
> —Winston Churchill

What if you turned failure into a stepping stone to success, instead of viewing it as something to be avoided at all costs?

Before I experienced my first real estate market crash, I thought I had it made. In only four years, I had turned less than $10,000 of my own money into more than $6,000,000 in real estate. I was on track to be able to retire by the time I was 31!

Then, everything changed.

Overnight, the value of my properties dropped in half. My company's revenue, which also revolved around real estate, dried up almost instantly. Suddenly, I couldn't pay my bills.

I was depressed and anxious and would cry uncontrollably for hours on end. I struggled to make ends meet. Finally, I was forced to declare bankruptcy.

I felt like a failure.

My long-time mentor, Fredric Lehrman, shared this with me, "I remember when Donald Trump went through the same thing. This is part of the process, PJ. It's just your turn. That's all."

Walt Disney went bankrupt several times. Thomas Edison experimented with over 6,000 materials to use as a filament in a light bulb before he found one that worked. Winston Churchill failed sixth grade and was defeated in every single election for public office until he became prime minister at the age of 62.

If success is the destination, what if experiencing failure is how you get there?

Through the process of losing everything and being forced to declare bankruptcy, I developed deep levels of humility and compassion for other people. I became a better investor and a better teacher. I redesigned my business in a way that would allow me to lead a happier and more balanced life. And my business is now more than *triple* what it was before the market crashed.

When you fail, that's when you learn the most. That's when you're at your most creative and resourceful. When you "lose," don't lose the lesson. When you fail, remind yourself that you have just taken one more step toward success.

How to Manifest More of What You Want

"What you focus on expands."
—Fredric Lehrman

Beliefs are thoughts that you continue to think, and are reinforced by evidence. These beliefs create your reality.

The more evidence you gather to support a particular belief, the stronger that belief becomes, and the quicker you create that reality for yourself.

Start by entertaining the idea that money comes to you easily and naturally. Money comes to you in unexpected ways for the good of all concerned. Everywhere you go, you find money on the ground. You regularly receive unexpected checks in the mail. An insurance refund. A friend sending you money. Stock you didn't remember you owned. A referral fee you weren't expecting.

There may be a part of your mind that resists this idea. If so, your mind isn't ready to accept this belief. So plant it like a seed in your mind, to grow into a thought, a belief, a reality. At that point, it will have become part of your life and part of who you are.

Imagine inviting a new friend over for a cup of tea. Invite her into your kitchen. Offer her a seat. Sit with her and listen. Appreciate her. Be with her.

Be with this new thought like you would be with a guest in your home. Entertain the idea that money comes to you easily and naturally. Examine and appreciate that idea.

Then look for evidence. A coin on the ground. A check in the mail. And when that evidence comes…

MILK IT FOR ALL IT'S WORTH!

Make a big deal out of it, even if all that happened was that you found a penny on the ground. Declare out loud, "I am a money magnet! Thank you! Thank you! Thank you!"

Celebrate. Tell everyone you know. If the people in your life think you're crazy, tell me. Go to www.RealProsperityInc.com and post your story as a comment on my blog.

Revel in that energy and that emotional state of celebration and gratitude as long as possible. Then look for even more evidence.

What's Next?

Thank you for reading the *Little Book of Prosperity*. I recommend that you keep it someplace where you will see it frequently, like your car, desk or bathroom. Open the book at random. That chapter is your message for the day.

These ideas and tools serve as a reminder for you to continue the practices of creating wealth and expanding your prosperity consciousness.

When you're ready for more great information, enjoy the special report I've created, "The Top 5 Keys to Financial Success."

This report is based on nine years of intense research and study with some of the most brilliant teachers and business owners in the world. I've distilled that knowledge into the five most essential keys an entrepreneur can have to create more money with less stress.

You can get your own free copy of my report. It is my gift to you. Just go to the Website listed at the back of the book.

Thank you!

Love and Prosperity,

PJ

Quoted Authors

Ben Stein

(1944-) Actor, writer, lawyer, and commentator on political and economic issues.

Dale Carnegie

(1888-1955) Pioneer in public speaking and personal development.

Doris Day

(1922-) American actress, singer, and animal rights activist.

Elbert Hubbard

(1856-1915) American writer, publisher, artist, and philosopher.

Eric Butterworth

(1913-2003) Popular Unity minister and author.

Fredric Lehrman

Director of Nomad University, creator of "Prosperity Consciousness" audio series, active in the field of business psychology for over 25 years.

George S. Clason

(1874-1957) Soldier, businessman and writer, best known for writing a series of informational pamphlets about being thrifty and how to achieve financial success that became *The Richest Man in Babylon.*

Henry Ford

(1863-1947) The founder of the Ford Motor Company and father of modern assembly lines that are used in mass production.

Karen Kingston

Pioneered the development of Space Clearing, the Feng Shui art of clearing and consecrating spaces in buildings, and is recognized as the Western world's leading authority in this field.

Mark Victor Hansen

(1948-) Inspirational and motivational speaker, trainer and author, best known as the founder and co-creator of the *Chicken Soup for the Soul* book series.

Oprah Winfrey

(1954-) Popular television talk show host, actor and producer.

Raymond Aaron

Success and investment coach, author of *Double Your Income Doing What You Love.*

Robert Kiyosaki

(1947-) Investor, businessman, author and motivational speaker, best known for his *Rich Dad, Poor Dad* series.

T. Harv Eker

Motivational speaker, touring lecturer and bestselling author.

Wayne Dyer

(1940-) Internationally renowned author and speaker in the field of self-development.

William Carleton

(1794-1869) Irish novelist.

Winston Churchill

(1874-1965) British politician known chiefly for his leadership of the United Kingdom during World War II.

PJ Recommends

Prosperity Consciousness (Audio Series) Fredric Lehrman

Rich Dad, Poor Dad Robert Kiyosaki

Double Your Income Doing What You Love Raymond Aaron

The Law of Attraction Michael J. Losier

The Richest Man in Babylon George S. Clason

Pay Yourself First Greg Etherton

Fail Better Herter Studio

Positive Words, Powerful Results Hal Urban

Ask and It Is Given Esther & Jerry Hicks (The Teachings of Abraham)

The One-Minute Millionaire Mark Victor Hansen and Robert Allen

About PJ Van Hulle:

PJ Van Hulle acquired over $6,000,000 in real estate in four years, created a six-figure seminar company, and was on track to be able to retire by the time she was 31. Then the real estate market crashed, and everything changed. After losing millions of dollars, she learned first hand that MAKING MONEY and KEEPING MONEY were two entirely different skill sets. Since then, PJ has rebounded, taking her company's sales to triple what they were before, and through her seminars and programs, has become even more passionate about providing people with the financial education they never received in school.

Thank You for Reading
The Little Book of Prosperity!

I have a gift for you:

"The Top 5 Keys to Financial Success"

This report is based on nine years of intense research and study with some of the most brilliant teachers and business owners in the world. I've condensed that knowledge to the five most essential keys to making more money with less stress.

Get your copy here:

www.littlebookfreegift.com